Congressional Research Service

How FDA Approves Drugs and Regulates Their Safety and Effectiveness

Susan Thaul
Specialist in Drug Safety and Effectiveness

June 25, 2012

Congressional Research Service

7-5700

www.crs.gov

R41983

CRS Report for Congress ———————————————

Prepared for Members and Committees of Congress

Summary

Update: On June 20, 2012, the House of Representatives passed, by voice vote and under suspension of the rules, S. 3187 (EAH), the Food and Drug Administration Safety and Innovation Act, as amended. This bill would reauthorize the FDA prescription drug and medical device user fee programs (which would otherwise expire on September 30, 2012), create new user fee programs for generic and biosimilar drug approvals, and make other revisions to other FDA drug and device approval processes. It reflects bicameral compromise on earlier versions of the bill (S. 3187 [ES], which passed the Senate on May 24, 2012, and H.R. 5651 [EH], which passed the House on May 30, 2012). The following CRS reports provide overview information on FDA's processes for approval and regulation of drugs:

- CRS Report R41983, *How FDA Approves Drugs and Regulates Their Safety and Effectiveness*, by Susan Thaul.

- CRS Report RL33986, *FDA's Authority to Ensure That Drugs Prescribed to Children Are Safe and Effective*, by Susan Thaul.

- CRS Report R42130, *FDA Regulation of Medical Devices*, by Judith A. Johnson.

- CRS Report R42508, *The FDA Medical Device User Fee Program*, by Judith A. Johnson.

(Note: The rest of this report has not been updated since September 1, 2011.)

The Food and Drug Administration (FDA) is a regulatory agency within the Department of Health and Human Services. A key responsibility is to regulate the safety and effectiveness of drugs sold in the United States. FDA divides that responsibility into two phases: *preapproval* (premarket) and *postapproval* (postmarket). FDA reviews manufacturers' applications to market drugs in the United States; a drug may not be sold unless it has FDA approval. The agency continues its oversight of drug safety and effectiveness as long as the drug is on the market. Beginning with the Food and Drugs Act of 1906, Congress has incrementally refined and expanded FDA's responsibilities regarding drug approval and regulation.

The progression to drug approval begins before FDA involvement. First, basic scientists work in the laboratory and with animals; second, a drug or biotechnology company develops a prototype drug. That company must seek and receive FDA approval, by way of an investigational new drug (IND) application, to test the product with human subjects. Those tests, called clinical trials, are carried out sequentially in Phase I, II, and III studies, which involve increasing numbers of subjects. The manufacturer then compiles the resulting data and analysis in a new drug application (NDA). FDA reviews the NDA with three major concerns: (1) safety and effectiveness in the drug's proposed use; (2) appropriateness of the proposed labeling; and (3) adequacy of manufacturing methods to assure the drug's identify, strength, quality, and identity. The Federal Food, Drug, and Cosmetic Act (FFDCA) and associated regulations detail the requirements at each step. FDA uses a few special mechanisms to expedite drug development and the review process when a drug might address an unmet need or a serious disease or condition. Those mechanisms include accelerated approval, animal efficacy approval, fast track applications, and priority review.

Once a drug is on the U.S. market (following FDA approval of the NDA), FDA continues to address drug production, distribution, and use. Its activities, based on ensuring drug safety and effectiveness, address product integrity, labeling, reporting of research and adverse events, surveillance, drug studies, risk management, information dissemination, off-label use, and direct-to-consumer advertising, all topics in which Congress has traditionally been interested.

FDA seeks to ensure product integrity through product and facility registration; inspections; chain-of-custody documentation; and technologies to protect against counterfeit, diverted, subpotent, adulterated, misbranded, and expired drugs. FDA's approval of an NDA includes the drug's labeling; the agency may require changes once a drug is on the market based on new information. It also prohibits manufacturer promotion of uses that are not specified in the labeling. The FFDCA requires that manufacturers report to FDA adverse events related to its drugs; clinicians and other members of the public may report adverse events to FDA. The agency's surveillance of drug-related problems, which had primarily focused on analyses of various adverse-event databases, is now expanding to more active uses of evolving computer technology and linking to other public and private information sources.

The FFDCA allows FDA to require a manufacturer to conduct postapproval studies of drugs. The law specifies when FDA must attach the requirement to the NDA approval and when FDA may issue the requirement after a drug is on the market. To manage exception risks of drugs, FDA may require patient or clinician guides and restrictions on distribution. The agency publicly disseminates information about drug safety and effectiveness; and regulates the industry promotion of products to clinicians and the public.

Contents

Figures

Tables

Contacts

T he Food and Drug Administration (FDA) oversees the approval and regulation of drugs entering the U.S. market. Two regulatory frameworks support the FDA's review of prescription drugs. First, FDA reviews the safety and effectiveness of new drugs that manufacturers wish to market in the United States; this process is called *premarket approval* or *preapproval review*. Second, once a drug has passed that threshold and is FDA-approved, FDA acts through its *postmarket* or *post-approval* regulatory procedures.

Update: On June 20, 2012, the House of Representatives passed, by voice vote and under suspension of the rules, S. 3187 (EAH), the Food and Drug Administration Safety and Innovation Act, as amended. This bill would reauthorize the FDA prescription drug and medical device user fee programs (which would otherwise expire on September 30, 2012), create new user fee programs for generic and biosimilar drug approvals, and make other revisions to other FDA drug and device approval processes. It reflects bicameral compromise on earlier versions of the bill (S. 3187 [ES], which passed the Senate on May 24, 2012, and HR 5651 [EH], which passed the House on May 30, 2012). The following CRS reports provide overview information on FDA's processes for approval and regulation of drugs:

- CRS Report R41983, *How FDA Approves Drugs and Regulates Their Safety and Effectiveness*, by Susan Thaul.

- CRS Report RL33986, *FDA's Authority to Ensure That Drugs Prescribed to Children Are Safe and Effective*, by Susan Thaul.

- CRS Report R42130, *FDA Regulation of Medical Devices*, by Judith A. Johnson.

- CRS Report R42508, *The FDA Medical Device User Fee Program*, by Judith A. Johnson.

(Note: The rest of this report has not been updated since September 1, 2011.)

This report is a primer on drug approval and regulation: it describes (1) how drugs are approved and come to market, including FDA's role in that process and (2) FDA and industry roles once drugs are on the pharmacy shelves.

Legislative History of Drug Regulation

Derived from the Dutch word meaning *to boast (quacken)*, "quack" is the word Americans have commonly used to describe charlatans in medicine. Quacks peddled adulterated and mislabeled medicines throughout the United States without penalty until 1906, when Congress passed the Food and Drugs Act,[1] one section of which outlawed the practice.

Over the next half-century, Congress passed two major pieces of legislation expanding FDA authority. It passed the Federal Food, Drug, and Cosmetic Act (FFDCA)[2] in 1938, requiring that drugs be proven safe before they could be sold in interstate commerce. Then, in 1962, in the wake of deaths and birth defects from the tranquilizer thalidomide marketed in Europe, Congress passed the Kefauver-Harris Drug Amendments to the FFDCA,[3] increasing safety provisions and requiring that drugs be proven effective as well.

Congress has amended the FFDCA many times, leading to FDA's current mission of assuring Americans that the medicines they use do no harm and actually work—that they are, in other

---

[1] Federal Food and Drug Act of 1906 (F&DA), P.L. 59-384, 1906.

[2] Federal Food, Drug, and Cosmetic Act (FFDCA), P.L. 75-717, 1938. The FFDCA included a provision to repeal the F&DA.

[3] Kefauver-Harris Drug Amendments to the FFDCA, P.L. 87-781, 1962.

words, *safe and effective*. In recent decades Congress has passed additional laws to boost pharmaceutical research and development and to speed the approval of new medicines.[4]

FDA also regulates products other than drugs—for example, biological products, medical devices, dietary supplements, foods, cosmetics, animal drugs, and tobacco products. Sometimes the agency addresses issues that straddle two or more product types that the law treats differently.

Textbox 1. Examples of Drug Laws that Amended the FFDCA

- The 1983 Orphan Drug Act, which provided incentives for pharmaceutical manufacturers to develop drugs, biotechnology products, and medical devices for the treatment of rare diseases and conditions;

- the 1984 Hatch-Waxman Act, a compromise balancing greater patent protection of manufacturers with quicker pub ic access to lower-priced generic drugs;

- the 1992 Prescription Drug User Fee Act (PDUFA), which ushered in user fees and performance goals for faster drug approvals;

- the 1997 FDA Modernization Act (FDAMA), which relaxed clinical testing requirements, eased access to experimental therapies, and awarded drugmakers six more months of marketing protection for testing drugs in pediatric patients.

- the 2002 Public Health Security and Bioterrorism Preparedness and Response Act, which reauthorized the FDAMA pediatric testing provision within the 2002 Best Pharmaceuticals for Children Act (BPCA) and extended the drug user fee law for five more years;

- the 2003 Pediatric Research Equity Act (PREA), which required manufacturers to include pediatric assessments in new drug applications; and

- the 2007 Food and Drug Administration Amendments Act (FDAAA), which went beyond the anticipated reauthorization of PDUFA, BPCA, and PREA (among other provisions) by also expanding FDA authority to regulate drug safety.[5]

How FDA Approves New Drugs

To market a prescription drug in the United States, a manufacturer needs FDA approval.[6] To get that approval, the manufacturer must demonstrate the drug's safety and effectiveness according to criteria specified in law and agency regulations, ensure that its manufacturing plant passes FDA inspection, and obtain FDA approval for the drug's labeling—a term that includes all written

---

[4] For a chronological listing of legislation relating to FDA regulation of drugs, see "Table 3. Human Drugs Statutory Authorities in 1980 and 2007" in CRS Report RL34334, *The Food and Drug Administration Budget and Statutory History, FY1980-FY2007*, coordinated by Judith A. Johnson.

[5] The Orphan Drug Act (P.L. 97-414), the Hatch-Waxman Act (the Drug Price Competition and Patent Term Restoration Act of 1984, P.L. 98-417), PDUFA (P.L. 102-571), FDAMA (P.L. 105-115), the Best Pharmaceuticals for Children Act (107-109), the Public Health Security and Bioterrorism Preparedness Act (P.L. 107-188), and the FDA Amendments Act of 2007 (FDAAA, P.L. 110-85).

[6] FDA-approved drugs are designated by law into only two categories: prescription and nonprescription (also referred to as over-the-counter). No drug was prescription-only until the 1951 Humphrey-Durham amendments [P.L. 82-215, the Food, Drug, and Cosmetics Act Amendments Act, 1951], which stated, "A drug intended for use by man which ... because of its toxicity or other potentiality for harmful effect, or the method of its use, or the collateral measures necessary to its use, is not safe for use except under the supervision of a practitioner licensed by law to administer such drug;" (FFDCA 503(b)(1)).

material about the drug, including, for example, packaging, prescribing information for physicians, and patient brochures.

The approval process begins before the law requires FDA involvement. **Figure 1** illustrates a product's timeline both before and during FDA involvement.

The research and development process for a finished drug usually begins in the laboratory. Basic research is often conducted or funded by the federal government.[7] When basic research yields an idea that someone identifies as a possible drug component, government or private research groups focus attention on a prototype design. At some point, private industry (either a large, established company or a newer, smaller, start-up company) continues to develop the idea, eventually testing the drug in animals. When the drug is ready for testing in humans, the FDA must get involved.

Figure 1. Drug Development Path

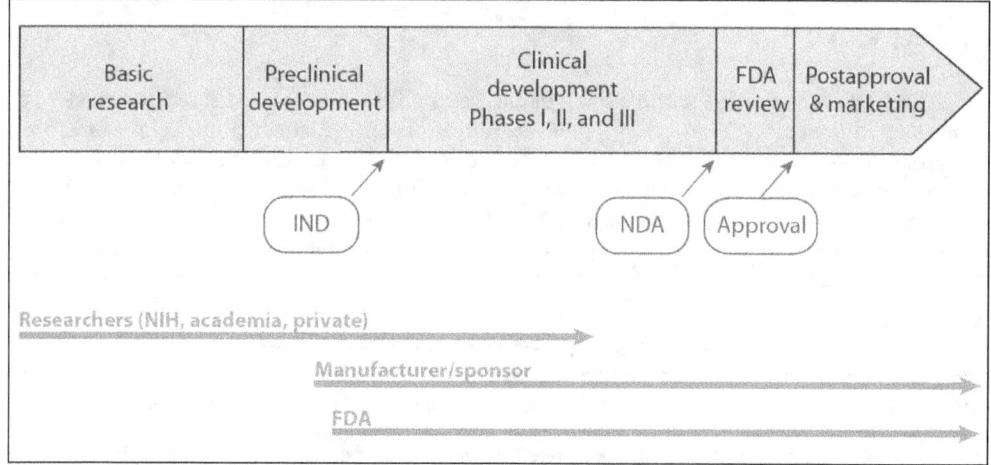

Source: Created by CRS.

Note: FDA = Food and Drug Administration. IND = investigational new drug app ication. NDA = new drug application.

The Standard Process of Drug Approval

The four FDA steps leading to the agency's approval of a new drug for marketing in the United States are described below. This report describes the process for a *new drug*. For a *generic drug*— one that is chemically and therapeutically identical to an already approved drug—the process is abbreviated.[8]

---

[7] CRS Report R41705, *The National Institutes of Health (NIH) Organization, Funding, and Congressional Issues*, by Judith A. Johnson and Pamela W. Smith, provides a definition ("basic research is research in the fundamental medical sciences, sometimes called lab or bench research, while clinical research involves patients") and a discussion of its relationship to drug development and clinical research.

[8] FDA, "Abbreviated New Drug Application (ANDA): Generics," http://www.fda.gov/Drugs/ DevelopmentApprovalProcess/HowDrugsareDevelopedandApproved/ApprovalApplications/ AbbreviatedNewDrugApplicationANDAGenerics/default.htm.

Investigational New Drug (IND) Application

Except under very limited circumstances, FDA requires data from clinical trials—formally designed, conducted, and analyzed studies of human subjects—to provide evidence of a drug's safety and effectiveness. Before testing in humans—called *clinical testing*—the drug's sponsor (usually its manufacturer) must file an investigational new drug (IND) application with FDA. The IND includes information about the proposed clinical study design, completed animal test data, and the lead investigator's qualifications. It must also include the written approval of an Institutional Review Board, which has determined that the study participants will be made aware of the drug's investigative status and that any risk of harm will be necessary, explained, and minimized. The application must include an "Indication for Use" section that describes what the drug does and the clinical condition and population for which the manufacturer intends its use. Trial subjects should be representative of that population. The FDA has 30 days to review an IND application. Unless FDA objects, a manufacturer may then begin clinical testing.

Clinical Trials

With IND status, researchers test in a small number of human volunteers the safety they had demonstrated in animals. These trials, called *Phase I clinical trials*, attempt, in FDA's words, "to determine dosing, document how a drug is metabolized and excreted, and identify acute side effects." If the sponsor considers the product still worthy of investment, it continues with *Phase II and Phase III clinical trials*. Those trials gather evidence of the drug's efficacy and effectiveness in larger groups of individuals with the particular characteristic, condition, or disease of interest, while continuing to monitor safety.[9]

Textbox 2. Safety, Efficacy, and Effectiveness

Safety is often measured by toxicity testing to determine the highest tolerable dose or the optimal dose of a drug needed to achieve the desired benefit. Studies that look at safety also seek to identify any potential adverse effects that may result from exposure to the drug. *Efficacy* refers to whether a drug demonstrates a health benefit over a placebo or other intervention when tested in an ideal situation, such as a tightly controlled clinical trial. *Effectiveness* describes how the drug works in a real-world situation. Effectiveness is often lower than efficacy because of interactions with other medications or health conditions of the patient, sufficient dose or duration of use not prescribed by the physician or followed by the patient, or use for an off-label condition that had not been tested.[10]

New Drug Application (NDA)

Once a manufacturer completes the clinical trials, it submits a new drug application (NDA) to FDA's Center for Drug Evaluation and Research (CDER). The NDA contains not only the clinical trial results, but also information about the manufacturing process and facilities, including quality control and assurance procedures. The application includes a product description (chemical formula, specifications, pharmacodynamics, and pharmacokinetics[11]); the indication (specifying

---

[9] FDA, "Inside Clinical Trials: Testing Medical Products in People; What Is a Clinical Trial?" Information for Consumers, http://www.fda.gov/Drugs/ResourcesForYou/Consumers/ucm143531.htm.

[10] A resource for epidemiologic terms is *A Dictionary of Epidemiology, Fifth Edition*, Miquel Porta, editor, Oxford University Press, 2008.

[11] "Pharmacokinetic [PK] studies provide information on what the body does to a drug. More specifically, it covers how a drug is absorbed, distributed, metabolized and eliminated by the body. Pediatric PK studies are generally (continued...)

one or more diseases or conditions for which the drug would be used and the population who would use it); labeling; manufacturing description; and a proposed Risk Evaluation and Mitigation Strategy (REMS), if appropriate.

During the NDA review, CDER officials evaluate the drug's safety and effectiveness data, analyze samples, inspect the facilities where the finished product will be made, and check the proposed labeling for accuracy.

FDA Review

FDA considers three overall questions in its review of an NDA:[12]

- Whether the drug is safe and effective in its proposed use, and whether the benefits of the drug outweigh the risks.

- Whether the drug's proposed labeling (package insert) is appropriate, and what it should contain.

- Whether the methods used to manufacture the drug and the controls used to maintain the drug's quality are adequate to preserve the drug's identity, strength, quality, and purity.

FDA scientific and regulatory personnel consider the application and prepare written assessments in several categories, including Medical, Chemistry, Pharmacology, Statistical, Clinical, Pharmacology, Biopharmaceutics, Risk Assessment and Risk Mitigation, Proprietary Name, and Label and Labeling.

The FFDCA requires "substantial evidence" of drug safety and effectiveness.[13] FDA has interpreted this term to mean that the manufacturer must provide at least two adequate and well-controlled Phase III clinical studies, each providing convincing evidence of effectiveness.[14] The agency, however, exercises flexibility in what it requires as evidence.[15] As its regulations describe in detail, FDA can assess safety and effectiveness in a variety of ways, relying on combinations of studies by the manufacturer and reports of other studies in the medical literature.[16] For many NDAs, FDA convenes advisory panels of experts to review the clinical data.[17] While not bound

---

(...continued)

performed in patients, and focus on the measurement of drug in blood, urine, or in other body fluids or tissues.... Pharmacodynamic [PD] studies provide information on what a drug does to the body. PD examines how a drug works in the body and the amount of drug needed to provide an effect" (FDA, "Pediatric Studies Characteristics," http://www.fda.gov/ScienceResearch/SpecialTopics/PediatricTherapeuticsResearch/ucm221758.htm).

[12] FDA, "New Drug Application (NDA): Introduction," http://www.fda.gov/Drugs/DevelopmentApprovalProcess/HowDrugsareDevelopedandApproved/ApprovalApplications/NewDrugApplicationNDA/default.htm.

[13] FFDCA (P.L. 75-717, 1938), §505(c) and (d).

[14] The requirements for adequate and well-controlled studies are given in 21 CFR 314.126.

[15] See FDA, *Guidance for Industry Providing Clinical Evidence of Effectiveness for Human Drug and Biological Products*, CDER and CBER, May 1998, at http://www.fda.gov/cder/guidance/1397fnl.pdf.

[16] The requirements for adequate and well-controlled studies are given in 21 CFR 314.126.

[17] FDA has established various advisory committees whose members advise the agency. Most are named and have duties in relation to an area of medicine (such as the Cardiovascular and Renal Drugs Advisory Committee), and some reflect cross-cutting issues (such as the Pediatric Advisory Committee and the Drug Safety and Risk Management Advisory Committee); see FDA, "Committees & Meeting Materials," http://www.fda.gov/AdvisoryCommittees/
(continued...)

---

by an advisory panel's recommendation regarding approval, FDA usually follows advisory panel recommendations.

FDA approves an application based on its review of the clinical and nonclinical research evidence of safety and effectiveness, manufacturing controls and facility inspection, and labeling. An approval may include specific conditions, such as required post-approval studies (or post-approval clinical trials, sometimes referred to as *Phase IV clinical trials*) that the sponsor must conduct after marketing begins. An approval may also include restrictions on distribution, required labeling disclosures, or other elements of Risk Evaluation and Mitigation Strategies (REMS), which are described below in the section titled "How FDA Regulates Approved Drugs."

FDA has 180 days to review an NDA. If it finds deficiencies, such as missing information, the clock stops until the manufacturer submits the additional information. If the manufacturer cannot respond to FDA's request (e.g., if a required study has not been done, making it impossible to evaluate safety or effectiveness of the drug), the manufacturer may voluntarily withdraw the application. If and when the manufacturer is able to provide the information, the clock resumes and FDA continues the review.

When FDA makes a final determination, it sends the applicant a "complete response letter."[18] If FDA decides to not approve an application, regulations state that the letter must describe the specific deficiencies the agency identified and recommend ways for the applicant to make the application viable. An unsuccessful applicant may request a hearing.[19] Regulations identify the reasons for which FDA can reject an NDA, which include problems with clinical evidence of safety and effectiveness for its proposed use, manufacturing facilities and controls, labeling, access to facilities or testing samples, human subject protections, and patent information.[20]

Special Mechanisms to Expedite the Development and Review Process

Not all reviews and applications follow the standard procedures. For drugs that address unmet needs or serious diseases or conditions, FDA regularly uses three formal mechanisms to expedite the development and review process:[21]

(...continued)

CommitteesMeetingMaterials/default.htm.

[18] Until July 2008, FDA responded to applicants with a letter indicating whether the application was "approved," "approvable" (pending specified additions, such as more testing, made to the application), or "unapprovable" (FDA, "Action Packages for NDAs and Efficacy Supplements," MAPP 6020.8, Manual of Policies and Procedures, Office of New Drugs, Center for Drug Evaluation and Research, Effective Date: November 13, 2002, http://www.fda.gov/downloads/AboutFDA/CentersOffices/CDER/ManualofPoliciesProcedures/UCM082010.pdf). In July 2008, FDA issued the rules regarding the "complete response letter " (FDA, 21 CFR Parts 312, 314, 600, and 601 [Docket No. FDA–2004–N–0510] (formerly Docket No. 2004N–0267), "Applications for Approval to Market a New Drug; Complete Response Letter; Amendments to Unapproved Applications; Final rule," *Federal Register*, v. 73, no. 133, July 10, 2008, pp. 39588- 39611).

[19] 21 CFR 314.110. Complete response letter to the applicant.

[20] 21 CFR 314.125. Refusal to approve an application.

[21] For a discussion of their use, intended effects, and statutory and regulatory bases, see CRS Report RS22814, *FDA Fast Track and Priority Review Programs*, by Susan Thaul.

- *Accelerated approval*[22] and *animal efficacy approval*[23] change what is needed in an application.

- *Fast track applications*[24] affect the timing and smoothness of the application process.

- *Priority review*[25] affects the timing of the review, not the process leading to submission of an application. (See **Textbox 3** for brief descriptions of these mechanisms.)

Textbox 3. Accelerated Approval, Fast Track, and Priority Review

Accelerated approval. FDA regulations allow "accelerated approval" of a drug or biologic product that provides a "meaningful therapeutic benefit ... over existing treatments." The rule covers two situations. The first allows approval to be based on c inical trials that, rather than using standard outcome measures such as survival or disease progression, use "a surrogate endpoint that is reasonably ikely ... to predict clinical benefit." The second situation addresses drugs whose use FDA considers safe and effective only under set restrictions that could include limited prescribing or dispensing. FDA usually requires postmarketing studies of products approved this way.

Fast track. The Food and Drug Administration Modernization Act of 1997 (FDAMA, P.L. 105-115) directed the Secretary to create a mechanism whereby FDA could designate as "Fast Track" certain products that meet two criteria. First, the product must concern a serious or life-threatening condition; second, it must have the potential to address an unmet medical need. Once FDA grants a Fast Track designation, it encourages the manufacturer to meet with the agency to discuss development plans and strategies before the formal submission of an NDA. Such early interaction can help clarify elements of clinical study design and presentation that if absent at NDA submission could delay approval decisions. However, FDA makes similar interactions available to any sponsor who seeks FDA consultation throughout the stages of drug development.

Priority review. Unlike Fast Track or Accelerated Approval, the Priority Review process begins only when a manufacturer officially submits an NDA. Priority Review, therefore, does not alter the timing or content of steps taken in a drug's development or testing for safety and effectiveness. Although Priority Review is not explicitly required by law, FDA has estab ished it in practice, and various statutes, such as the Prescription Drug User Fee Act (PDUFA), refer to and sometimes require it. When FDA determines that a product would address an unmet need, it places it through Priority Review. That designation results in an average turnaround time (from completed app ication to approval decision) of approximately 6 months, rather than the 10-month average for Standard Review.

---

[22] 21 CFR 314 Subpart H.

[23] The Animal Efficacy Rule allows manufacturers to submit effectiveness data from animal studies as evidence to support applications of certain new products "when adequate and well-controlled clinical studies in humans cannot be ethically conducted and field efficacy studies are not feasible" (21 CFR 314 Subpart I and 21 CFR 601 Subpart H).

[24] FFDCA §506 [21 USC §356]. FDA, "Guidance for Industry: Fast Track Drug Development Programs—Designation, Development, and Application Review," Center for Drug Evaluation and Research and Center For Biologics Evaluation and Research, January 2006.

[25] FDA Center for Drug Evaluation and Research, Manual of Policies and Procedures 6020 3, revised July 18, 2007; FDA Center for Biologics Evaluation and Research, Manual of Standard Operating Procedures and Policies 8405, revised September 20, 2004; FDA, "FY 2010 Performance Report to the President and Congress for the Prescription Drug User Fee Act," http://www.fda.gov/downloads/AboutFDA/ReportsManualsForms/Reports/UserFeeReports /PerformanceReports/ PDUFA/UCM243358.pdf; and FDA, "Fast Track, Accelerated Approval and Priority Review," http://www.fda.gov/ForConsumers/ByAudience/ForPatientAdvocates/SpeedingAccesstoImportantNewTherapies/ ucm128291.htm. Congress used the Priority Review mechanism to encourage the development of treatments for tropical diseases; FFDCA §524 allows the Secretary to issue a transferable priority review voucher "to the sponsor of a tropical disease product application that entitles the holder of such voucher to priority review of a single human drug application."

Other options fit limited situations and support shorter times from idea to approved public use. For example, the Project BioShield Act of 2004 allows the HHS Secretary to authorize in certain circumstances the *emergency use* of products that do not yet have FDA approval.[26]

How FDA Regulates Approved Drugs

FDA's role in ensuring a drug's safety and effectiveness continues after the drug is approved and it appears on the market. FDA acts through its *postmarket regulatory procedures* after a manufacturer has sufficiently demonstrated a drug's safety and effectiveness for a defined population and specified conditions and the drug is *FDA-approved*. Manufacturers *must* report all serious and unexpected adverse reactions to FDA, and clinicians and patients *may* do so. FDA oversees surveillance, studies, labeling changes, and information dissemination, among other tasks.

FDA Offices Responsible for Drug Postapproval Regulation

Offices throughout FDA, mostly in the Center for Drug Evaluation and Research, address the safety of the drug supply. The primary focus of activity is the Office of Surveillance and Epidemiology (OSE), formerly named the Office of Drug Safety. Other organizational units evaluating safety issues include the Office of Regulatory Affairs; the Division of Drug Marketing, Advertising and Communications; the Division of Drug Information; and the Division of Compliance Risk Management and Surveillance.

OSE uses reports of adverse events that consumers, clinicians, or manufacturers believe might be drug-related to "identify drug safety concerns and recommend actions to improve product safety and protect the public health."[27] FDA activities regarding drug safety once a drug is on the market (postmarket or postapproval period) are diverse. FDA staff

- look for "signals" of safety problems of marketed drugs by reviewing adverse event reports through the MedWatch program;

- review studies conducted by manufacturers when required as a condition of approval;

- monitor relevant published literature;

- conduct studies using computerized databases;

- review errors related to similarly named drugs;

- conduct communication research on how to provide balanced benefit and risk information to clinicians and consumers; and

- remain in contact with international regulatory bodies.

---

[26] 21 USC 360bbb-3.

[27] FDA, "Office of Surveillance and Epidemiology (OSE)," CDER, http://www.fda.gov/AboutFDA/CentersOffices/CDER/ucm106491.htm.

Among the many advisory groups that work with FDA, two have roles specific to drug safety. The Drug Safety and Risk Management Advisory Committee met for the first time with this name in July 2002.[28] Members, appointed by the commissioner, represent areas of expertise in science, risk communication, and risk management. The group "advises the Commissioner or designee in discharging responsibilities as they relate to helping to ensure safe and effective drugs for human use."[29] One member may be designated to represent consumer concerns; one non-voting member may represent industry concerns.[30]

FDA created the Drug Safety Oversight Board as part of its 2005 Drug Safety Initiative and later required by FDAAA.[31] Its members include both FDA personnel and representatives of the Agency for Healthcare Research and Quality, the Centers for Disease Control and Prevention, the Department of Defense, the Indian Health Service, the National Institutes of Health, and the Department of Veterans Affairs.[32] Its roles are to advise the CDER director "on the handling and communicating of important and often emerging drug safety issues" and to provide "a forum for discussion and input about how to address potential drug safety issues."[33]

FDA Drug-Regulation Activities

FDA postmarket drug safety and effectiveness activities address aspects of drug production, distribution, and use. This section highlights nine activities that have traditionally interested Congress in relation to drug safety and effectiveness: product integrity, labeling, reporting, surveillance, drug studies, risk management, information dissemination, off-label use, and direct-to-consumer advertising.

---

[28] A predecessor group was the Drug Abuse Advisory Committee (http://www.fda.gov/OHRMS/DOCKETS/98fr/071102f.htm).

[29] FDA, "Drug Safety and Risk Management Advisory Committee Charter," http://www.fda.gov/AdvisoryCommittees/CommitteesMeetingMaterials/Drugs/DrugSafetyandRiskManagementAdvisoryCommittee/ucm094886 htm.

[30] FDA, "Drug Safety and Risk Management Advisory Committee," http://www.fda.gov/AdvisoryCommittees/CommitteesMeetingMaterials/Drugs/DrugSafetyandRiskManagementAdvisoryCommittee/default.htm. Holding joint meetings with disease-focused advisory committees (e.g., Anesthetic and Life Support Drugs; Arthritis; Endocrinologic and Metabolic Drugs; and Pulmonary-Allergy Drugs Advisory Committees), the Drug Safety and Risk Management Advisory Committee considered varied topics in 2010, including new drug applications for the treatment of fibromyalgia; the relief of moderate to severe pain where the use of an immediate-release, orally administered, opioid analgesic tablet is appropriate; the results of studies evaluating the addition of niacin, added for the purpose of reducing the misuse of oxycodone; and a non-steroidal anti-inflammatory drug product indicated for the treatment of the signs and symptoms of osteoarthritis. Other topics included a proposed Risk Evaluation and Mitigation Strategy for extended-release and long-acting opioid analgesics; the cardiovascular safety of a drug approved for blood glucose control in adults with type 2 diabetes mellitus; and the design of medical research studies to evaluate serious asthma outcomes with the use of the class of asthma medications known as long-acting beta-2 adrenergic agonists.

[31] FDAAA §901(b) added FFDCA §505-1(j).

[32] FDA, "Drug Safety Oversight Board," http://www.fda.gov/AboutFDA/CentersOffices/CDER/ucm082129 htm. Examples of topics the DSOB considered in 2010 are proton pump inhibitors and the risk of fractures; gadolinium-based contrast agents and renal adverse events and anaphylaxis; CT scans, radiation exposure, and cancer risk; bisphosphonates and a potential risk of atypical femoral shaft fracture; opioid REMS for extended-release and long-acting products; genetic testing for cisplatin-induced ototoxicity; issues surrounding the heparin potency change; how to communicate FDA's updated recommendations about long acting beta agonists (LABAs); and the propoxyphene safety issue.

[33] FDA, "Drug Safety Oversight Board," http://www.fda.gov/AboutFDA/CentersOffices/CDER/ucm082129 htm.

Product Integrity

Ensuring product integrity[34] was the key task of FDA's predecessors. It is still an essential concern of the agency. The FFDCA dictates requirements that manufacturers must meet, and it allows FDA to regulate manufacturing facilities, warehouses, and transportation plans.[35] For example, among many other requirements, the FFDCA requires (1) annual registration of "any establishment in any State engaged in the manufacture, preparation, propagation, compounding, or processing of a drug or drugs";[36] (2) submission of lists of products, including ingredients and labeling;[37] (3) inspection of drug lots for packaging and labeling control;[38] and (4) "sampling and testing of in-process materials and drug products."[39]

One way to track product integrity is a chain-of-custody document, defined by an FDA official as a record of "the movement of the drug from the place of manufacture through the U.S. drug supply chain to the final dispenser."[40] Such a document would allow someone to take a drug off the pharmacy shelf and determine where it was mixed and manufactured, what ships or trucks transported it, and who was responsible each time the finished product or its ingredients changed hands. Since 1987, Congress has required that a statement accompany each transfer of a finished drug, identifying the date and entity of each prior transfer (sale, purchase, transfer).[41] Although implementing regulations have been delayed in court cases, manufacturers do create chain-of-custody documents and FDA has presented its requirements in a Compliance Policy Guide.[42]

FDAAA added that the Secretary must develop standards and identify and validate effective technologies to secure the drug supply chain against counterfeit, diverted, subpotent, standard, adulterated, misbranded, or expired drugs. FDAAA directed the Secretary, in developing those standards, to address promising technologies, such as radiofrequency identification technology, nanotechnology, encryption technologies, and other track-and-trace technologies.

FDAAA also mandated that the Secretary develop a standardized numerical identifier to be applied to a prescription drug at the point of manufacturing and repackaging; undertake enhanced and joint enforcement activities with other federal and state agencies; and establish regional

[34] FFDCA section titles refer to "adulterated" (§501) and "misbranded" (§502) drugs.

[35] Although this discussion focuses on U.S. facilities, the FFDCA includes registration and product listing requirements for foreign facilities involved with drugs FDA-approved for sale in the United States. FDA and others are looking at how the agency carries out its regulatory responsibilities in an increasingly global industry (see, for example, FDA, "Report to Committee on Appropriations: Report on FDA's Approach to Medical Product Supply Chain Safety in response to the Joint Explanatory Statement to accompany H.R. 1105, the Omnibus Appropriations Act, 2009," July 2009, http://www.fda.gov/downloads/Safety/SafetyofSpecificProducts/UCM184049.pdf).

[36] FFDCA §510(b) [21 USC 310(b)] and 21 CFR Part 207.

[37] FFDCA §510(j) [21 USC 360(j)] and 21 CFR Part 207.

[38] 21 CFR 211.134.

[39] 21 CFR 211.110.

[40] Statement of Randall W. Lutter, Ph.D., Associate Commissioner for Policy and Planning, Food and Drug Administration, before the Subcommittee on Criminal Justice, Drug Policy, and Human Resources, House Committee on Oversight Government Reform, "Pharmaceutical Supply Chain Security," July 11, 2006, http://www.fda.gov/NewsEvents/Testimony/ucm111440.htm.

[41] Prescription Drug Marketing Act of 1987 (PDMA).

[42] FDA, "Compliance Policy Guide: CPG Sec. 160.900 Prescription Drug Marketing Act—Pedigree Requirements under 21 CFR Part 203," http://www.fda.gov/ICECI/ComplianceManuals/CompliancePolicyGuidanceManual/ucm073857.htm.

capabilities for validation and inspection. In March 2010, FDA published guidance on standardized numerical identification.[43]

Labeling

Adverse events sometimes warrant regulatory actions such as labeling changes, letters to health professionals, or, once in a great while, a drug's withdrawal from the market. The regulations require a company to make the label change as soon as there is reasonable evidence—not proof—of an *association* with serious hazard.[44]

Textbox 4. Example: Same Data, Different Decisions

The art and science of these judgments result, at times, in different decisions by different reviewers. An interesting example appeared on FDA's website on February 9, 2005, regarding Adderall, a stimulant medication used to treat attention deficit disorder. On the basis of data from U.S. reporting systems, Canadian authorities chose to stop sales, whereas U.S. authorities chose to alert the public but not to restrict sales at that time.[45] One year later, however, the FDA Drug Safety and Risk Management Advisory Committee reviewed data that "suggested stimulants might increase the risks of strokes and serious arrhythmias in children and adults" and recommended that FDA "require manufacturers to provide written guides to patients and place prominent warnings on drug labels describing these risks."[46]

Researchers debate the effectiveness of labeling. This is particularly true when it comes to black-box warnings, so called because they are bordered in black to signify their importance. A 2006 study of physician compliance with the warnings found that when prescribing drugs with black-box warnings, doctors violated those warnings in 7% of prescriptions.[47]

FDA can institute label changes based on information it gathers from mandatory industry reports to its Adverse Events Reporting System (AERS), manufacturer-submitted postmarket studies, and voluntary adverse event reports from clinicians and patients. When a manufacturer believes data from original or published studies support a new use for a drug, a manufacturer itself can initiate a label change to support a new marketing claim. The manufacturer submits to FDA the new data in a supplement to the original NDA and requests that FDA allow it to modify the labeling. In addition, if a manufacturer wants to strengthen warning labeling, it may do so before FDA approves that supplemental application.[48] With FDAAA, the Secretary may, upon learning of new relevant safety information, require a labeling change.

---

[43] FDA, "Guidance for Industry: Standards for Securing the Drug Supply Chain - Standardized Numerical Identification for Prescription Drug Packages," Office of the Commissioner (OC), Center for Drug Evaluation and Research (CDER), Center for Biologics Evaluation and Research (CBER), Office of Regulatory Affairs (ORA), March 2010, http://www.fda.gov/downloads/RegulatoryInformation/Guidances/UCM206075.pdf.

[44] 21 CFR 201.57(e).

[45] FDA, "Statement on Adderall," *FDA Statement*, February 9, 2005, at http://www.fda.gov/bbs/topics/news/2005/NEW01156.html, and FDA, Public Health Advisory for Adderall and Adderall XR, February 9, 2005, at http://www.fda.gov/cder/drug/advisory/adderall.htm.

[46] Gardiner Harris, "Warning Urged on Stimulants Like Ritalin," *New York Times*, February 10, 2006; and FDA, CDER, Draft Agenda, Drug Safety and Risk Management Advisory Committee, Gaithersburg, Md., February 9-10, 2006, at http://www.fda.gov/ohrms/dockets/ac/06/briefing/2006-4202B1_03_FDA-Tab03.pdf.

[47] Karen E. Lasser, Diane L. Seger, D. Tony Yu, et al., "Adherence to Black Box Warnings for Prescription Medications in Outpatients," *Archives of Internal Medicine*, vol. 166, February 13, 2006, pp. 338-344.

[48] FDA, "Supplemental Applications Proposing Labeling Changes for Approved Drugs, Biologics, and Medical (continued...)

Labeling plays a major role in the presentation of safety and effectiveness information. Some contend that changes in prescribing information are not enough to protect the public's health because, as recent questions from consumers and Members of Congress demonstrate, the labeling language, clear to those in the drug approval business, can confuse lay readers. For example, "Studies in children have not demonstrated effectiveness" represents a different state of knowledge than "Effectiveness in children has not been demonstrated." The first sentence says that researchers have looked to see whether the drug was effective and were unable to find that evidence—although the drug still could be effective in children, the study design or analysis did not see that. The second sentence, however, does not clarify whether any study had been done.

In January 2006, FDA issued a final rule, final guidance, and supporting documents to overhaul the labeling requirements for prescription drugs.[49]

Reporting

Once FDA approves a drug, it monitors safety. Manufacturers *must* report all serious and unexpected adverse reactions to FDA's Adverse Events Reporting System (AERS) within 15 days of becoming aware of them (21 CFR 310.305). Health professionals and patients *may* report adverse reactions to FDA's MedWatch reporting system at any time. FDA adds MedWatch submissions to the AERS database.[50] A manufacturer must also report the results of clinical studies it conducts on its approved products, along with what it knows about others' research and publications.[51]

Surveillance

FDA gathers information about possible adverse reactions to the products it has approved for U.S. use. Under the authority granted by FFDCA, FDA requires manufacturers to report adverse events. It also provides a procedure for consumers and physicians to voluntarily report their concerns about drugs. The agency collects those reports through MedWatch and uses its Adverse Event Reporting System (AERS)[52] to store and analyze them. Because some events may occur after the use of a drug for reasons unrelated to the it, FDA scientists review the events to assess which ones may indicate a drug problem. They then use information gleaned from the surveillance data to determine a course of action. They might recommend a change in drug

---

(...continued)

Devices; Final rule," *Federal Register*, v. 73, no. 164, August 22, 2008, pp. 49603-49610.

[49] See the FDA News release for links to various documents, at http://www.fda.gov/NewsEvents/Newsroom/PressAnnouncements/2006/ucm108579.htm.

[50] FDA presents quarterly summaries of AERS data on its website (FDA, "Adverse Event Reporting System (AERS) Statistics," http://www.fda.gov/Drugs/GuidanceComplianceRegulatoryInformation/Surveillance/AdverseDrugEffects/ucm070093.htm). The agency also makes raw AERS data available to the public, although it notes that "[U]sers of these files need to be familiar with creation of relational databases using applications such as ORACLE®, Microsoft Office Access, MySQL® and IBM DB2 or the use of ASCII files with SAS® analytic tools. ... A simple search of AERS data cannot be performed with these files by persons who are not familiar with creation of relational databases" (FDA, "The Adverse Event Reporting System (AERS): Latest Quarterly Data Files," http://www.fda.gov/Drugs/GuidanceComplianceRegulatoryInformation/Surveillance/AdverseDrugEffects/ucm082193.htm).

[51] FFDCA §505(k).

[52] FDA, "MedWatch: The FDA Safety Information and Adverse Event Reporting Program," http://www.fda.gov/Safety/MedWatch/default.htm; and FDA "Adverse Event Reporting System (AERS)," http://www.fda.gov/Drugs/InformationOnDrugs/ucm135151.htm.

---

labeling to alert users to a potential problem, or, perhaps, to require the manufacturer to study the observed association between the drug and the adverse event.

Unlike planned studies with hypotheses to support or refute, for which researchers gather information, most surveillance activities are characterized as *passive*, in that the information is submitted by others.[53] The agency only learns of an adverse event when someone reports one. FDA is aware of the limitations of that approach. The reported event may signal a problem with the drug or be unrelated but have occurred coincident with the dosing. Other actual drug effects may be unrecognized as such and consequently not be reported. In addition, it is difficult to interpret the extent of a problem without knowing how many people took a specific drug.

In 2008, both recognizing these limitations and responding to a requirement in FDAAA to create and maintain a Postmarket Risk Identification and Analysis System,[54] FDA began work on its Sentinel Initiative to move from its predominantly passive surveillance system to an active one. Building on surveillance activities already in place, and using evolving computer technology, FDA has started to develop an infrastructure that uses data from public and private sources, protects confidentiality, and expands its information base. By setting up the Sentinel System to coordinate many different automated data systems, FDA aims to better detect safety signals, analyze data to understand them, and identify strategies to fix the problem.[55]

Drug Studies

After a drug is on the market, FDA can recommend and ask product sponsors to conduct studies, but in only limited situations does the law authorize FDA to *require* studies in the postapproval period. Two sets of situations—distinguished by when the requirement is set—involve required postapproval studies: when a requirement is attached to the initial approval of the drug and when FDA informs the sponsor of a required study once a drug is on the market.

Postmarket Studies Required upon Drug Approval

Accelerated Approval. When FDA grants accelerated approval, it attaches a postmarket study requirement to that approval. Regulations state, "Approval under this section will be subject to the requirement that the applicant study the drug further, to verify and describe its clinical benefit, where there is uncertainty as to the relation of the surrogate endpoint to clinical benefit, or of the observed clinical benefit to ultimate outcome."[56]

---

[53] CDC describes four types of surveillance methods, with the passive method's being predominant. "The term passive is used to convey the idea that health authorities take no action while waiting for report forms to be submitted" (CDC, "Methods of Surveillance," Program Operations Guidelines for STD Prevention, Surveillance and Data Management, August 16, 2007, http://www.cdc.gov/std/program/surveillance/4-PGsurveillance.htm#passive).

[54] FDAAA §905(a) amended FFDCA §505(k) to require the Secretary to, among other things, "use electronic health data for risk identification and analysis; provide standardized reporting of adverse event data; and use federal, private, and other data sources to conduct active adverse event surveillance and identify trends and patterns." A fuller description is in CRS Report RL34465, *FDA Amendments Act of 2007 (P.L. 110-85)*, by Erin D. Williams and Susan Thaul.

[55] Sentinel Initiative, http://www.fda.gov/Safety/FDAsSentinelInitiative/ucm203500.htm, and http://www.fda.gov/Safety/FDAsSentinelInitiative/default.htm, FDA, "The Sentinel Initiative: A National Strategy for Monitoring Medical Product Safety," May 2008, http://www.fda.gov/Safety/FDAsSentinelInitiative/ucm089474.htm and http://www.fda.gov/downloads/Safety/FDAsSentinelInitiative/UCM124701.pdf.

[56] 21 CFR 314.510.

Animal Efficacy. When FDA grants approval based on its animal efficacy rule, it attaches a postmarket study requirement to that approval. The Animal Efficacy Rule allows manufacturers to submit effectiveness data from animal studies as evidence to support applications of certain new products "when adequate and well-controlled clinical studies in humans cannot be ethically conducted and field efficacy studies are not feasible."[57] The regulations state,

> The applicant must conduct postmarketing studies, such as field studies, to verify and describe the drug's clinical benefit and to assess its safety when used as indicated when such studies are feasible and ethical. Such postmarketing studies would not be feasible until an exigency arises.... Applicants must include as part of their application a plan or approach to postmarketing study commitments in the event such studies become ethical and feasible.[58]

Pediatric Assessments. When FDA approves a drug for which it has deferred the required pediatric assessment, it attaches a postmarket pediatric assessment requirement to that approval. With the Pediatric Research Equity Act (PREA, P.L. 108-155, reauthorized in P.L. 110-85), Congress required manufacturers to submit a pediatric assessment with each submission of an application to market a new active ingredient, new indication, new dosage form, new dosing regimen, or new route of administration.[59] The law specified situations in which the Secretary might defer or waive the pediatric assessment requirement. For a deferral, an applicant must include a timeline for completion of studies. The Secretary must review each approved deferral annually, for which the applicant must submit evidence of documentation of study progress.

Postmarket Studies Required After Drug Approval

Pediatric Assessment. PREA allows the Secretary to require that the manufacturer of an approved drug submit a pediatric assessment in certain circumstances.[60]

Based on New Information Available to Secretary. The Secretary, under specified conditions after a drug is on the market, may *require* a study or a clinical trial.[61] The Secretary may determine the need for such a study or trial based on newly acquired information. To require a postapproval study or trial, the Secretary must determine that (1) other reports or surveillance would not be adequate and (2) the study or trial would assess a known serious risk or signals of serious risk, or identify a serious risk. The law directs the Secretary regarding dispute resolution procedures.

Risk Management

With authority under the FFDCA or by practice, FDA has long implemented various tools in its attempt to ensure that the drugs it has approved for marketing in the United States are safe and effective for their intended and approved uses. Although the agency requires certain actions of the

---

[57] 21 CFR 314 Subpart I and 21 CFR 601 Subpart H.

[58] 21 CFR 314.610.

[59] PREA provisions are generally codified in FFDCA §505B [21 USC 355c] Research Into Pediatric Uses for Drugs and Biological Products. See CRS Report RL33986, *FDA's Authority to Ensure That Drugs Prescribed to Children Are Safe and Effective*, by Susan Thaul, for a description of the law's requirements and a discussion of the issues.

[60] FFDCA §505B [21 USC 355c].

[61] These provisions are in FFDCA §505(o) [21 USC 355(o)] New Drugs; Postmarket studies and clinical trials; labeling.

manufacturers[62] of all approved drugs, it deems additional actions appropriate for specific drugs or specific circumstances surrounding a drug's use. Some of those actions are risk-management processes to identify and minimize risk to patients. The FDA *Manual of Policies and Procedures* notes that risk management attempts to "minimize [a drug's] risks while preserving its benefits."[63] In that 2005 document, which is still in effect, FDA described its approach to risk management as "an iterative process" that includes both risk assessment and risk minimization. Actions available to FDA include

- education and outreach (e.g., new professional labeling, patient-oriented labeling, public notices);

- guides to prescribing, dispensing, or use (e.g., informed consent, program enrollment, practitioner certification, special packaging, and limited refills);

- restricted access (e.g., registration of physicians, pharmacists, or patients, and documentation of laboratory tests before dispensing); and

- suspension or termination of product marketing.[64]

Textbox 5. Balancing Risks and Benefits

The balance of a drug's risks and benefits is not always clear. For example, FDA implemented a risk-minimization plan for Accutane (isotretinoin), a drug that treats a severe type of acne and carries with it a risk of birth defects and possible suicidal actions. Some clinicians objected to what they felt were onerous prescribing requirements, saying that those requirements serve to deny the drug to individuals who need it.[65] FDA allowed an exception, for example, for oncologists prescribing isotretinoin for cancer treatment.[66]

The Food and Drug Administration Amendments Act of 2007 (FDAAA, P.L. 110-85) named the risk-management process the Risk Evaluation and Mitigation System (REMS) and expanded the risk-management authority of FDA.[67] FDA practice has long included most of the elements that a REMS may include. FDAAA gave FDA, through the REMS process, the authority for structured follow-through, dispute resolution, and enforcement.[68]

---

[62] The Federal Food, Drug, and Cosmetic Act refers to the sponsor of an application or the holder of an approved application. Because that entity is often the product's manufacturer or its employee, this memorandum uses the term *manufacturer* throughout. Note that the manufacturer may also be the responsible person, for purposes of enforcement.

[63] FDA, "Review Management: Risk Management Plan Activities in OND and ODS," *Manual of Policies and Procedures*, MAPP 6700.1, CDER (Originator: Office of New Drugs), effective September 8, 2005, http://www.fda.gov/downloads/AboutFDA/CentersOffices/CDER/ManualofPoliciesProcedures/ucm082058.pdf.

[64] Toni Piazza-Hepp, FDA presentation: "Risk Management Programs," at the Risk Management Public Workshop, CDER, Washington, D.C., April 10, 2003, at http://www.fda.gov/cder/meeting/RMtranscript2.doc; and FDA, *Center for Drug Evaluation and Research 2004 Report to the Nation Improving Public Health Through Human Drugs*, August 2005, at http://www.fda.gov/cder/reports/rtn/2004/rtn2004.pdf.

[65] Gardiner Harris, "System Said to Fail to Steer Women From Acne Drug," *New York Times*, February 11, 2006.

[66] "FDA Announcement Re: iPledge Program for Isotretinoin," memorandum from Richard Pazdur, Div. of Oncology Drug Products, CDER, at http://www.ons.org/fda/documents/fda050306.pdf; and FDA, "FDA and Manufacturers of Accutane and its Generics to Implement iPLEDGE Program on March 1, 2006," *FDA Statement*, February 23, 2006, at http://www.fda.gov/bbs/topics/NEWS/2006/NEW01324.html.

[67] The REMS authority is in FFDCA §505-1 (21 USC 355-1). REMS are discussed in the presentation of Title IX (Enhanced Authorities Regarding Postmarket Safety of Drugs) of FDAAA, pages 68-78, including Tables 12 and 13, in CRS Report RL34465, *FDA Amendments Act of 2007 (P.L. 110-85)*, by Erin D. Williams and Susan Thaul. FDAAA also covered many other issues.

[68] FDA has issued draft guidance documents for industry on REMS: FDA, DRAFT "Guidance for Industry: Format and (continued...)

FDA may require a REMS under specified conditions—including if it determines such a strategy is necessary to ensure that the benefits of a drug outweigh its risks. It may make the requirement when a manufacturer submits a new drug application, after initial approval or licensing, when a manufacturer presents a new indication or other change, or when the agency becomes aware of new information and determines a REMS is necessary.[69]

As part of a REMS, the Secretary may require instructions to patients and clinicians, and restrictions on distribution or use (and a system to monitor their implementation). As listed in FFDCA Section 505-1 (21 USC 355-1), a REMS may include the following components:

Patient information. The manufacturer must develop material "for distribution to each patient when the drug is dispensed."[70] This could be a Medication Guide, "as provided for under part 208 of title 21, Code of Federal Regulations (or any successor regulations),"[71] or a patient package insert.

Health care provider information. The manufacturer must create a communication plan, which could include sending letters to health care providers; disseminate information to providers about REMS elements to encourage implementation or explain safety protocols; or disseminate information through professional societies about any serious risks of the drug and any protocol to assure safe use.

Elements to assure safe use (ETASU). An ETASU is a restriction on distribution or use that is intended to (1) allow access to those who could benefit from the drug while minimizing their risk of adverse events and (2) block access to those for whom the potential harm would outweigh potential benefit. By including these restrictions, FDA can approve a drug that it otherwise would have to keep off the market because of the risk it would pose. FFDCA Section 505-1(f)(3) lists the types of restrictions FDA could require.

- health care providers who prescribe must have particular training or experience, or be specially certified;

(...continued)

Content of Proposed Risk Evaluation and Mitigation Strategies (REMS), REMS Assessments, and Proposed REMS Modifications," Center for Drug Evaluation and Research (CDER) and Center for Biologics Evaluation and Research (CBER), September 2009, http://www.fda.gov/downloads/Drugs/GuidanceComplianceRegulatoryInformation/ Guidances/UCM184128.pdf; and FDA, DRAFT "Guidance for Industry: Medication Guides—Distribution Requirements and Inclusion in Risk Evaluation and Mitigation Strategies (REMS)," CDER and CBER, February 2011, http://www.fda.gov/downloads/ Drugs/GuidanceComplianceRegulatoryInformation/Guidances/UCM244570.pdf.

[69] As of July 8, 2011, FDA had established 190 REMS for individual drugs. These are listed in FDA, "Approved Risk Evaluation and Mitigation Strategies (REMS)," http://www.fda.gov/Drugs/DrugSafety/PostmarketDrugSafety Information for PatientsandProviders/ucm111350 htm. In addition to drug-specific individual REMS, FFDCA §505-1 authorizes FDA to require a REMS for all the drugs in a pharmacological class and sets out required steps that include public meetings (which could include the product sponsors, advisory committees, expert workshops, etc.), announcement in the *Federal Register* of planned regulatory action, and public comment. FDA has completed this process for a class-wide REMS for long-acting and extended-release opioid products (FDA, "Opioid Drugs and Risk Evaluation and Mitigation Strategies (REMS)," http://www.fda.gov/Drugs/DrugSafety/InformationbyDrugClass/ ucm163647.htm; and FDA, "Questions and Answers: FDA Requires a Risk Evaluation and Mitigation Strategy (REMS) for Long-Acting and Extended-Release Opioids," http://www.fda.gov/Drugs/DrugSafety/ InformationbyDrugClass/ucm251752.htm).

[70] FFDCA §505-1(e)(2).

[71] FFDCA §505-1(e)(2)(A).

- pharmacies, practitioners, or health care settings that dispense must be specially certified;

- the drug must be dispensed to patients only in certain health care settings, such as hospitals;

- the drug must be dispensed to patients with evidence or other documentation of safe-use conditions, such as laboratory test results;

- each patient using the drug must be subject to certain monitoring; and

- each patient using the drug must be enrolled in a registry.

Any approved REMS must include a timetable of when the manufacturer will provide reports to allow FDA to assess the effectiveness of the REMS components.

Information Dissemination

FDA maintains several communications channels through which it distributes information on drug safety and effectiveness to clinicians, consumers, pharmacists, and the general public. These include a monthly *Drug Safety Newsletter*,[72] *Drug Safety Communications*,[73] *FDA Drug Safety Podcasts*,[74] *FDA Drug Info Rounds*,[75] and *FDA Drug Information on Twitter*.[76]

FDAAA required FDA to establish an Advisory Committee on Risk Communication to "advise the Commissioner on methods to effectively communicate risks associated with" FDA-regulated products. It also added important items to the ways that FDA informs the public about information it has developed or gathered about drug safety and effectiveness. One required report to Congress must address how best to communicate risks and benefits of new drugs to the public and "the role of the risk evaluation and mitigation strategy in assessing such risks and benefits."[77] The report may also consider whether FDA, when determining the labeling of a new product or use for a product, should alert the public that the agency's approval is based on limited clinical trials that may not have identified all possible risks associated with the drug—risks that may become evident when patients use the new drug in community (rather than experimental) settings or when the number of users becomes large enough to yield rare drug effects. Any published direct-to-consumer prescription drug advertisement must include a statement encouraging the reporting of negative side effects to FDA, along with a 1-800 number and website address. Finally, FDAAA required that, after studying the issue, the Secretary report to Congress whether that statement is appropriate for television advertisements as well. The Secretary informed

---

[72] FDA, "Drug Safety Newsletter," http://www.fda.gov/Drugs/DrugSafety/DrugSafetyNewsletter/default.htm and http://www.fda.gov/Drugs/DrugSafety/DrugSafetyNewsletter/ucm096049.htm.

[73] FDA, "Drug Safety Communications," http://www.fda.gov/drugs/drugsafety/ postmarketdrugsafetyinformationforpatientsandproviders/ucm199082.htm.

[74] FDA, "FDA Drug Safety Podcasts," http://www.fda.gov/Drugs/DrugSafety/DrugSafetyPodcasts/default.htm.

[75] FDA, "FDA Drug Info Rounds," http://www.fda.gov/Drugs/ResourcesForYou/HealthProfessionals/ucm211957 htm.

[76] FDA, "FDA Drug Information (FDA_Drug_Info) on Twitter," http://twitter.com/FDA_Drug_Info.

[77] FDAAA §904. FDA submitted the report on August 31, 2009 (http://www.fda.gov/RegulatoryInformation/ Legislation/FederalFoodDrugandCosmeticActFDCAct/SignificantAmendmentstotheFDCAct/ FoodandDrugAdministrationAmendmentsActof2007/FDAAAImplementationChart/default.htm).

Congress in May 2008 that FDA is conducting a multi-year study of the content and placement of such a statement.[78]

Another FDAAA requirement is for the Secretary to screen the Adverse Event Reporting System (AERS) database on a bi-weekly basis and report quarterly on the AERS website regarding new safety information or potential signals of a serious risk, and to report to Congress on procedures for addressing ongoing postmarket safety issues identified by the Office of Surveillance and Epidemiology.

Other sections of FDAAA addressed communication with the public, expert committees, and others about agency actions and plans. The Secretary must develop and maintain a website with extensive drug safety information, and publish a list of all authorized generic drugs. The Secretary also must provide public access to action packages for product approval or licensure, including certain reviews, and establish an Advisory Committee on Risk Communication.

Off-Label Use

The FFDCA prohibits a manufacturer from promoting or advertising a drug for any use not listed in the FDA-approved labeling, which contains those claims for which FDA has reviewed safety and effectiveness evidence.[79] However, the FFDCA does not give FDA authority to regulate the practice of medicine; that responsibility rests with the states and medical professional associations. Once a drug is approved, a licensed physician may—except in highly regulated circumstances—prescribe it without restriction. A prescription to an individual whose demographic or medical characteristics differ from those indicated in a drug's FDA-approved labeling is called *off-label use* and is accepted medical practice.

Textbox 6. Examples of Off-Label Use

- A drug that was tested in an eight-week trial may be prescribed for long-term use.
- If a drug was tested at one dose, it may be used at higher or lower doses.
- A drug tested in adults may be prescribed to children.
- A drug tested for the treatment of one disease may be prescribed in an attempt to prevent another.

Off-label use presents an evaluation problem to FDA safety reviewers. Using drugs in new ways for which researchers have not yet demonstrated safety and effectiveness can create problems that premarket studies did not address. Manufacturers rarely design studies to establish the safety and

---

[78] FDA, "Report to Senate Committee on Health, Education, Labor, and Pensions and the House Committee on Energy and Commerce; Report on Study Commitment Regarding Inclusion of Toll-Free Adverse Event Reporting Number by FDA Food and Drug Administration," May 2008, http://www.fda.gov/downloads/RegulatoryInformation/Legislation/ FederalFoodDrugandCosmeticActFDCAct/SignificantAmendmentstotheFDCAct/FoodandDrugAdministrationAmend mentsActof2007/FDAAAImplementationChart/UCM147012.pdf; and FDA [Docket No. FDA-2008-N-0595], "Agency Information Collection Activities; Proposed Collection; Comment Request; Experimental Study: Toll-Free Number for Consumer Reporting of Drug Product Side Effects in Direct-to-Consumer Television Advertisements for Prescription Drugs," *Federal Register*, vol. 73, no. 229, November 26, 2008, pp. 72058-72062. See also: FDA 21 CFR Parts 201, 208, and 209 [Docket No. FDA–2003–N–0313] (formerly Docket No. 2003N–0342) RIN 0910–AC35, "Toll-Free Number for Reporting Adverse Events on Labeling for Human Drug Products; Final rule," *Federal Register*, vol. 73, no. 209, October 28, 2008, pp. 63886-63897.

[79] The line between promotion and professional education is not always clear. See CRS Report R40458, *FDA Guidance Regarding the Promotion of Off-Label Uses of Drugs Legal Issues*, by Vanessa K. Burrows and Kathleen Ann Ruane.

---

effectiveness of their drugs in off-label uses, and individuals and groups wanting to conduct such studies face difficulties finding funding.

Direct-to-Consumer Advertising

FDA regulates the advertising of prescription drugs.[80] Although the Federal Trade Commission regulates nonprescription drug advertising, the FDA regulates the product labeling that the nonprescription drug ads must reflect. FDAAA expanded and strengthened FDA's enforcement tools regarding advertising. The Secretary may now require submission of a television advertisement for review before its dissemination. Based on this review, during which the Secretary may consider the impact the drug might have on specific population groups (such as older and younger individuals, or racial and ethnic minorities), the Secretary may recommend, but not require, changes in the ad. The law authorizes the Secretary to require that an ad include certain disclosures without which the Secretary determines that the ad would be false or misleading. These disclosures concern information about a serious risk listed in a drug's labeling and the date of a drug's approval.

FDAAA required that television and radio ads present the required information on side effects and contraindications in a "clear, conspicuous, and neutral manner."[81] It also established civil penalties for the dissemination of a false or misleading direct-to-consumer (DTC) advertisement. Also, any published DTC advertisement must include the following statement printed in conspicuous text: "You are encouraged to report negative side effects of prescription drugs to the FDA. Visit http://www.fda.gov/medwatch, or call 1-800-FDA-1088."[82]

Author Contact Information

Susan Thaul
Specialist in Drug Safety and Effectiveness
sthaul@crs.loc.gov, 7-0562

---

[80] For an indepth discussion of this issue, see CRS Report R40590, *Direct-to-Consumer Advertising of Prescription Drugs*, by Susan Thaul.

[81] FFDCA §502(n) as amended by FDAAA §901(d)(3).

[82] FFDCA §502(n) as amended by FDAAA §906(a).

www.ingramcontent.com/pod-product-compliance
Lightning Source LLC
Chambersburg PA
CBHW082207290526
45794CB00008B/3451